Blind Faith

Blind Faith

*When faith without logic embraces evil without
boundaries, then there is no deception, no abhorrent act
or denial of reality that will not seek justification or
claim absolution in the name of God and send you
down the rabbit-hole to spiritual madness*

"When I get home I shall write
a book about this place"
- Alice -

BRIAN S. NEUMANN

Published by *Neu Creations Ministry*
326 South 28th Avenue | Brighton CO 80601 USA

Book design copyright © 2020 by *Brian S. Neumann*. All rights reserved.
Cover design by *Brian Neumann* (inspired by picture: Lewis Carroll; Ella birak - Alice in Wonderland / karen cox. The Look: "Escape from Wonderland" by Simon McCheung)

Interior design by *Brian Neumann*

Published in the United States of America
Religion / Christianity / Politics
ISBN: 978-164826209-8

Foreword

This book is about real-life *Alice* who, in blind faith, follows a *White Rabbit* down the proverbial *rabbit-hole* that leads her to a *Wonderland,* where, among other things, she ends up at a tea-party, hosted by a *Mad Hatter* and *March Hare* who incessantly fill her head with non-sensical, hallucinatory riddles and tales.

As she relentlessly continues trying to follow the White Rabbit, Alice makes acquaintances who give her strange advice and misleading directions until, finally, she ends up on trial for crimes that—in this real-life version—she really did commit.

This is the sad, sobering but true account of *Seventh-day Adventist's* and other entities who have chosen to follow a religious or political thought-leader down the rabbit-hole of specious dogmas and practices.

Dedication

For those who want to avoid the rabbit-hole of blind
faith and those who are trying to find their way out
—The truth will set you free—

Contents

Sources section at the end of the book

CHAPTER I

Down the Rabbit Hole

"It would be so nice if something made
sense for a change"

It would be impossible to comprehensively discuss America—its morals, values, political philosophy, national identity and laws—without examining the role that Christianity has played in its establishment and growth. This is especially true when one considers America's Protestant heritage, and, post Independence, the faiths that were birthed and the continued effect they have had on the Christian beliefs of its people.

I was poignantly reminded of this when I came across a recent article in the *New York Times* that sought to highlight the shift taking place among the younger generation of Evangelicals, provocatively titled, *"God is Going to Have to Forgive Me": Young Evangelicals Speak Out.*

The title immediately caught my attention, prompting me to ask: "would God ever have to forgive anyone for doing something that was in accordance with His will?" To me, as someone who understands the concept of sin and forgiveness, the answer seemed to be pretty self-evident. No. However, in case there was something in the article that might help me better understand what inspired the title, I decided to read further.

The author, *Elizabeth Dias*, opened with a paragraph that highlighted the current influence of evangelicalism on American politics:

> *The role of evangelical Christianity in American politics has been a hotly discussed topic this year, intersecting with front-burner issues like immigration, the Supreme Court and social justice. Often the loudest evangelical voices are white, male and ... not young.* [1]

Apparently, after spending "many hours interviewing respondents," she came to the following conclusions:

> *Young evangelicals are questioning the typical ties between evangelicalism and Republican politics. Many said it had caused schisms within their families. And many described a real struggle with an administration they see as hostile to immigrants, Muslims, L.G.B.T.Q. people, and the poor. They feel it reflects a loss of humanity, which conflicts with their spiritual call.* [2]

Dias reports that while these young Evangelicals agree that President Trump has "helped to achieve their biggest goals, like curbing abortion rights and advancing religious liberties ... they are still sensitive to other issues ..."

Issues of concern include, how the L.G.B.T.Q. and other "marginalised" communities, such as Muslims, are being treated. After reading the six interviews she published I came to the conclusion that, firstly, Dias is suggesting that the older generation of "white males" act contrary to the gospel of Christ while the younger generation, in their attitude, demonstrate a more Christ-like spirit.

What Dias is doing is creating a straw-man to bolster her essential argument that Evangelicals (White males) who share the perspective of the Trump administration on issues such as immigration, the L.G.B.T.Q. community, Muslims and other so-called minorities, are un-Christian.

Her mad-hatter argument however makes no sense because she avoids addressing the most important issue of all—the issue being that it does not really matter what she thinks. In fact, it does not matter what the older white male generation or the younger generation think either. What REALLY matters is what God thinks.

At the end of the day, all she is doing is playing the political game to create the impression that a "newer" more "revitalised" and "genuine" version of Christianity is actually starting to lean more towards non-sensical, leftist, democrat definitions of morals and values.

What she is most certainly right about is that there has been a shift in Christianity. Departure from conservative values has not only been in the secular, political arena. Christians from all denominational groups, in order to stay "relevant" in a rapidly changing world, have for many decades now been doing the same. It is thus totally bogus to measure Christian sincerity or Christ-like behavior on the basis of whether someone agrees that the L.G.B.T.Q. lifestyle should be seen as acceptable, rather than establishing whether Scripture— the blueprint for Judeo-Christian morality—determines it to be such. After all, one of the most basic tenants of

Biblical Christianity is that the believer "ought to obey God rather than men" (Acts 5:29).

Likewise, in the context of Old Testament instruction, *Isaiah* the prophet states: "To the law and to the testimony [God's instruction]: if they speak not according to this word, it is because there is no light in them" (Isaiah 8:20).

Following the command to stay true to scriptural standards is not a reflection on whether a genuine Christian, who expresses disagreement with a particular lifestyle or religious choice, truly loves their fellowman or not. Christ, for example, defended the prostitute that the Pharisees were planning to stone to death. However, his defense of her, which resulted in the hypocritical Pharisees not following through on the stoning, was not intended to indicate that Christ condoned prostitution— He still called it "sin." His parting words to the prostitute were consistent with the Divine standard (law and the testimony): "Neither do I condemn thee: go, and *sin no more*" (John 8:11).

The inconsistency with Judeo-Christian compromise becomes a dangerous problem when religious leaders, to keep favor with the general population or the powers that be, tweak or even deny the Divine standard— Scripture.

What becomes even more dangerous is when religious institutions, in order to achieve the ultimate goal of power for themselves, resort to manipulating the clear words of Scripture.

History has shown that any sort of religio-political dominance, barring the Hebrew dispensation, when Jehovah Himself was Supreme Authority in both spiritual and national concerns, always ended in disaster. Even in the Hebrew dispensation, when the Israelites demanded an earthly king and God granted their wish, it ended in national ruin.

The only time when monarchy and religion can work as co-ruling institutions, when perfect justice and mercy can be maintained, is when the Creator Himself is in the position of Supreme Authority.

Human leadership, although it may be under men of spiritual and religious bent, is nonetheless still human and prone to the bias of sin. This is why, such as was the case with those Founders of the American nation (the Framers of its Judeo-Christian Constitution and developers of its system of government), checks and balances were set in place to curb corruption by those in positions of power.

Religious entities have often exerted their influence in order to manipulate and control the masses, especially when a particular faith becomes the official religion of the state—which, when this ultimate status is reached, often leads to outright persecution. However, this also happens when a religious institution, without the support of the state, in order to manipulate its members and maintain a façade of exclusivity, claims to have God's special favor—the only true faith among all other faiths. In this type of scenario, the faith in question, more often than not, bolsterers its claims by providing some sort of extra-biblical, "divinely inspired" source of authority—such as a prophet.

Power does not only corrupt in the secular sphere. Power, especially when that power is absolute, corrupts in the religious sphere to no lesser degree. The record of history, and indeed the pages of Scripture, are replete with accounts of cruelty and abuse, practiced by men and woman in positions of religious influence.

In lieu of these facts, it is of vital importance to

consider the positive and negative impact of religious teaching on the thinking of American society in regard to morals, values and politics. This goes without saying, because religious beliefs directly influence the way people relate to their role in society, and how, in light of these beliefs, they exercise their vote and support the powers that be.

It is also true, because of the ever increasing influence of media and entertainment and the relentless efforts of the left to purge God and Christian faith from the public sphere, that American youth are being influenced less and less by those unequivocal Christian morals and values that guided the thinking of previous generations.

This trend, especially via the educational system, has opened the door to indoctrination of leftist, socialist ideology, which has resulted in a steady moral decline. In spite of this, there are a significant number of believers, albeit mostly among the older generation, whose thinking is still strongly influenced by their Christian, spiritual values.

In a country such as America, with its Judeo-Christian origins, some of the most insidious forms of political manipulation come from "exclusive" faiths, who, while they claim to teach essential, biblical truth, also promote ideas that cannot be scripturally substantiated and thus directly affect the way in which their members relate to the question of patriotism, politics and government.

Commonly, these kinds of entities encourage religious practices and beliefs, that if not accepted or adhered to, will risk members losing eternal salvation. When it comes to this kind of spiritual manipulation, I can say quite categorically, I have a lifetime of experience—born and raised, a fourth generation descendent of pastors, missionaries, evangelists and denominational workers in the *Seventh-day Adventist* (SDA) church.

In my mid teens, after being schooled in the SDA educational system, I left the church and for nearly 18 years pursued a career as a professional musician in the rock music industry. When I returned, in my mid 30's, I became an apologist and impassioned defender of SDA beliefs. Indeed, when it comes to the teachings and fabulous claims made by the SDA denomination, inspired by its leading founder and prophetess, *Ellen G. White*, I am a bonafide insider.

Of the numerous American-born faiths of the 19th Century, the SDA denomination has become one of the wealthiest, influential, and yet, least understood. Thus, while I have investigated all the American-born institutions of that era, who use some or other extra-biblical source to support their claims, I will here, for the purpose of making my point, focus exclusively on the SDA faith.

𝔖𝔢𝔳𝔢𝔫𝔱𝔥-𝔡𝔞𝔶 𝔄𝔡𝔳𝔢𝔫𝔱𝔦𝔰𝔪—"𝔍 𝔰𝔥𝔞𝔩𝔩 𝔢𝔩𝔲𝔠𝔦𝔡𝔞𝔱𝔢"

NOTE: For a far more comprehensive study on Seventh-day Adventism, its primary founder and prophetess, Ellen G. White, her plagiarism, false claims and unscriptural teachings, obtain a copy of my book: *The White Elephant —In Seventh-day Adventism.*

When one examines the SDA Church's relationship to government, from its birth, it becomes obvious that the attitude of membership, to everything from voting to political involvement, are directly tied to a variety of unscriptural teachings of the church—substantiated by the extra-biblical revelations of its prophetess, *Ellen G. White.*

In the context of the United States of America, this can be a rather complex and contradictory scenario, which non-Adventists, and at times even members, do not fully grasp. However, if one wants to properly understand the SDA relationship to government and politics, all one needs to do is examine its history, not only in America, but world-wide.

In America and elsewhere in the world, a significant number of SDA's choose not vote for any political party. In many cases there is an attitude of absolute non-involvement. In America specifically, when SDA's do choose to vote, the majority tend to lean Democrat, as testified to in the official SDA publication, *Adventist Review.* Indeed, the title of its 2016 March edition reads: *U.S. Adventists lean More Democrat Than Republican, Survey Finds.* [3]

When it comes to the leadership of the church however, whether from the *General Conference* (the leading body of the church), on down to divisions, conferences and local churches, etc., there have, historically, to varied degrees and in different countries, been compromises and collusion taking place between church leaders and the powers that be.

To better understand this, I will, throughout this book, examine three cases in point: SDA's in *Nazi Germany, Apartheid South Africa,* and, in a more secondary sense, *America,* the birth-place of the SDA movement. I will also, in order to reveal the primary source for that which motivates Adventist philosophy, highlight the specific, "divinely" inspired teachings of

Ellen G. White that have been at the very foundation of the question I will examine in this book.

When I specifically deal with the history of America, I will show how SDA teachings regarding America in end-time prophecy and Ellen G. White's "inspired" insight concerning voting and politics, in light of constitutional considerations, caused them to take a position that was based on blatant ignorance of the facts.

For now, and by way of introduction, I will share a brief history of the SDA denomination's origins in the mid 19th Century and certain scripturally untenable teachings that either put SDA's at odds with, or as the case might be, in alignment with practices of the state— at times, some of the most reprehensible governments and practices of the 19th and 20th Century.

"I'm late, I'm late! For a very important date! No time to say hello, goodbye,' I'm late, I'm late, I'm late!"

The SDA movement rose out of the ashes of *William Miller's* failed prediction that the world would end and Christ would return on *22 October, 1844*. This event is known in SDA circles as *The Great Disappointment*. However, while the event, for those Millerite Adventists (Millerite's) who were looking forward to it, failed to materialize, they very quickly— as is often the case with people who fervently believe in some predicted event that fails to occur—came up with an explanation that helped inspire a new movement which eventually became the SDA Church.

"𝕾𝖍𝖊 𝕯𝖔𝖊𝖘𝖓't 𝕶𝖓𝖔𝖜 𝖂𝖍𝖆𝖙 𝖆𝖓 𝖀𝖓𝖇𝖎𝖗𝖙𝖍𝖉𝖆𝖞 𝖎𝖘"

Based on a revelation that was given to a Millerite Adventist, *Hiram Edson,* the morning after the disappointment, and subsequent visions received by young oracle, *Ellen Harmon* (Ellen G. White), an explanation for this non-event was given. Instead of a visible second coming and end-world event, Christ had, according to the claimed revelations, actually passed from the Holy to the Most Holy apartment of the heavenly sanctuary to begin, what SDA's term the *Investigative Judgement.* This explanation satisfied the remnant group of adventists who still clung to the belief that something, anything, even if no one on the planet could actually prove it, did occur on the "unbirthday" of 22 October 1844.

Out of this disappointment, under the leadership of *Ellen Harmon, James White*—whom she married—and later *Joseph Bates* and other Adventist believers, developed a movement, that in a primary sense, was guided by Ellen's "prophetic gift."

Based on her revelations and unusual manipulation of numerous passages of Scripture, she and the early theologians, scholars and thought leaders of the group, set about establishing what were to become the foundational doctrines, or pillars of SDA faith.

"𝕱𝖔𝖗 𝖎𝖋 𝖔𝖓𝖊 𝖉𝖗𝖎𝖓𝖐𝖘 𝖒𝖚𝖈𝖍 𝖋𝖗𝖔𝖒 𝖆 𝖇𝖔𝖙𝖙𝖑𝖊 𝖒𝖆𝖗𝖐𝖊𝖉 'poison,' 𝖎𝖙'𝖘 𝖆𝖑𝖒𝖔𝖘𝖙 𝖈𝖊𝖗𝖙𝖆𝖎𝖓 𝖙𝖔 𝖉𝖎𝖘𝖆𝖌𝖗𝖊𝖊 𝖜𝖎𝖙𝖍 𝖔𝖓𝖊 𝖘𝖔𝖔𝖓𝖊𝖗 𝖔𝖗 𝖑𝖆𝖙𝖊𝖗"

It goes without saying that one of the first pillars of faith established by this fledgling group of Advent, Millerite believers, concerned the "unbirthday" of 22 October

1844 and what they were now proclaiming actually happened.

It is important to have some understanding of this because it is directly as a result of teachings connected to this doctrine that the belief in SDA exclusivity—God's only true body of faith on earth—was developed. Additionally, an understanding of these beginnings also provide the backdrop for understanding SDA's relationship to government and politics and their peculiar view of the American nation.

The Adventists of post 1844, who fanatically clung to this new insight concerning the disappointment, confirmed and guided by visions that Ellen White claimed were given her by God, began to see themselves as the *Little Flock*, or remnant body of true believers that God had specifically singled out as His chosen.

All the rest of the religious world who did not believe in their interpretation of the failed 1844 prediction were, according to Ellen White, the "fallen denominational churches"—essentially, the rest of the Christian world. Regarding the faithful Advent believers of their group, Ellen White wrote:

> *Those [the Advent believers] who, with a knowledge of the truth from the Scriptures, had also the Spirit and grace of God, and who,* **in the night of their bitter trial** *[the disappointment], had patiently waited,* **searching the Bible for clearer light,**—*these* **saw the truth concerning the sanctuary in Heaven and the Saviour's change of ministration** *[moving from the Holy to the Most Holy apartment], and* **by faith they followed him in his work** *in the sanctuary above.* [4]

During those early post-disappointment years Ellen White claimed that the door of mercy had been shut for the rest of the world and that even the religious revivals of other Christian churches were not genuine. Regarding this she wrote:

> *The excitements and false reformations of this day do not move us, for we know that **the Master of the house rose up in 1844, and shut the door of the first apartment of the heavenly tabernacle**; and now we certainly expect that **they will go with their flocks to seek the Lord; but they shall not find him; he hath withdrawn himself** [within the second veil] **from them**. The Lord has shown me that **the power that is with them is a mere human in influence** and not the power of God.* [5]

Concerning the other Christian faiths, who did not accept her interpretation of the disappointment and Christ moving from the Holy to the Most Holy, she gives this "inspired" description of them bowing before God's throne. Her claim was that, while they thought they were praying to God, they were, in fact, praying to Satan:

> *I turned to look at the company [Christians who did not accept the SDA interpretation of the failed Millerite prediction of 22 Oct, 1844] who were still **bowed before the throne** [in the holy]; they **did not know that Jesus had left it. Satan appeared to be by the throne, trying to carry on the work of God. I saw them look up to the throne, and pray, "Father, give us your Spirit." Satan would then breathe upon them an unholy influence**; in it there was light and much power, but no sweet love, joy, and peace. Satan's object was to keep them deceived and to draw back and deceive God's children.* [6]

It is on the basis of teachings such as this—which are only a sample of the many statements by Ellen White designating SDA's their special status among the rest of Christianity—that the SDA doctrine of exclusivity developed and still presently remains in vogue. For example, *SDA General Conference President, Ted Wilson*, leader of the SDA Church, in a sermon he delivered at the 2014 *Annual Council* on Oct 11th, in *Silver Spring, Maryland*, declared:

> *As Seventh-day Adventists at this 2014 Annual Council,* **we affirm without hesitation** *that* **God has given us** *a special mission for these closing hours of Earth's history, and the devil is furious...* **This prophetic movement** *[SDA Church], described in Revelation 12:17 as God's remnant people who "keep the commandments of God, and have the testimony of Jesus,"* **is constituted in ONLY one body of faith today: the Seventh-day Adventist Church** ... (emphasis supplied).

Thus, while the SDA Church strongly support separation of church and state and work "to protect the religious rights of all people of faith, no matter what their denominational affiliation,"[7] they still view other faiths as the "fallen denominational churches," that according to Ellen G. White, constitute "Babylon."

I can say, without doubt, because of my intimate familiarity with SDA mindset, that it suits them to take the position they do, because in standing up for the rights of ALL religions they, by default, protect their own interests as well.

As far as political involvement by its members is concerned, the SDA Church officially discourages it. In this regard SDA's are unlike Evangelicals and Catholics, who, on the whole, are much more active politically.

Although this position is partly due to SDA's skewed interpretation of separation of church and state—that Christians essentially have no business taking positions in favour of or against political parties—it is also a position spawned from statements by Ellen G. White that proclaim SDA's "chosen" status and their belief concerning the role of America in Bible prophecy.

In respect to SDA's getting involved in politics, she said, on behalf of God: "The Lord would have His people bury political questions." We cannot with safety vote for political parties." Let political questions alone. It is a mistake for you to link your interests with any political party, to cast your vote with them or for them."[8]

Rhetorically, she questioned: "Can Seventh-day Adventists participate in certain aspects of politics with good conscience? Are we ever to help in the making of laws, and if so, how? Is it ever proper to hold public office, either elective or appointive?"[9]

SDA Bible scholar, author of numerous volumes on SDA prophecy and theology, and editor of the official church publication, The *Review and Herald*, *Uriah Smith*, outlined the reasons for why SDA's do not get involved in political concerns:

> *To the question, why we do not with our votes and influence labor against the evil tendency of the times, we reply, that* **our views of prophecy lead us to the conclusion that things will not be bettered....***And we feel it our duty* **to confine our efforts to preparing ourselves, and others as far as in us lies, for the great and final issue already pressing upon us—the revelation of the Son [of] man from heaven, the destruction of all earthly governments,** *the establishment of the glorious, universal*

and eternal kingdom of the King of kings, and the redemption and deliverance of all His subjects.[10]

The reader will notice that the key reasons for not becoming politically involved, in voting or otherwise are, firstly, because of the SDA view of prophecy—specifically regarding America—which I will address shortly, and secondly, because casting one's vote, will apparently not help in bettering the situation, as all governments will ultimately be destroyed anyway.

My question to this sort of logic would be: "If you are not, as a Christian, prepared to get involved in helping make a better nation in this life—a nation established on Judeo-Christian principles—then what makes you think that you will even inherit the eternal kingdom that God is going to establish?"

Your first duty, as a Christian in this life, besides winning souls for Christ, is to contribute to making this world a better place—this is part of what it means to walk the Christian walk.

The issues that Ellen White and the church during that era encouraged casting one's vote for were for causes such as, the *prohibition movement, temperance reform* and *slavery*—things that one could argue were not overtly connected to any political cause.[11]

Since that time, SDA's have done all sorts of exegetical tap-dancing to get around the issue and legitimize some sort of involvement in party voting—in order to have at least some voice in the political sphere.

However, all of these attempts fly in the face of the categorical teachings of their prophetess and the original position of the church. In short, as it is with so much that SDA's do, they want to be able to say "we have the Spirit of Prophecy (manifest in their prophetess, Ellen G.

White), but we will pick and choose when, where and what we will obey—when it suits us." The hypocrisy, double-standard and contradiction in all of this will become more and more apparent as I continue.

"Curtsey while you're thinking. It saves time"

The prime source one needs to consult, in order to establish exactly what SDA's teach regarding America, is Ellen G. White. Indeed, all theories and ideas, whether of liberal or conservative SDA origin are subject to review by the *Biblical Research Institute* of the SDA Church—the official church body that determines whether any new interpretations of Scripture/SDA teachings are acceptable or not. Invariably, these will be evaluated, not only on the basis of the SDA interpretation of the Bible, but will also be compared to Ellen White's inspired insight. In the end, the prime authority, really ends up being Ellen White. The reason for this is simply that much of the detail of SDA end-time prophecy cannot be categorically verified by the Bible alone.

In light of these facts it is vital to know what Ellen White says about America in prophecy, particularly in reference to *Revelation 13:11, 12*—the second dragon-like beast, which forms a partnership with the first beast of that chapter whom Ellen White/SDA's believe is the Roman Catholic Church. In an official SDA daily devotional, *Maranatha,* Ellen White is quoted:

> *I beheld **another beast** [U.S.A] coming up out of the earth; and he had two horns like a lamb, and he spake as a dragon [Satan]. Rev. 13:11.*
> ***One nation, and only one, meets the***

specifications of this prophecy; it points unmistakably to the **United States of America.**

... The law of God, through the agency of Satan, is to be made void. In our land of boasted freedom, religious liberty will come to an end.

When our nation, in its legislative councils, shall enact laws to bind the consciences of men in regard to their religious privileges, enforcing Sunday observance [the mark of Roman Catholic authority]**, and bringing oppressive power to bear against those who keep the seventh-day Sabbath, the law of God will, to all intents and purposes, be made void in our land; and national apostasy will be followed by national ruin.**

... When **the leading churches of the United States, uniting upon such points of doctrine as are held by them in common, shall influence the state to enforce their decrees and to sustain their institutions, then Protestant America will have formed an image of the Roman hierarchy** [papal Rome]**,** and the infliction of civil penalties upon dissenters will inevitably result.[12]

In an oyster-shell, SDA's regard the United States as being the final governmental authority that will follow Satan, the Dragon, and then, as the world's leading power, it will give eventual religious control to the Pope (Rome) and will force the world, via a false religious awakening and then legislation, to keep Sunday holy. Those who refuse to obey, SDA's being the prime target, will be prosecuted under the law, and then, according to their extrapolation of *Revelation 13*, will receive the death penalty for their disobedience.

It is on the basis of all the above—commencing with the disappointment of 22 October 1844 and how the

SDA pioneers, under guidance of their prophetess, Ellen White, fashioned their teachings and vision of themselves—that SDA's still, in the 21st Century, have a natural bent to distrust government, especially conservatives, because they believe that this end-time scenario will be initiated, not by the liberal left, but by the conservative right—Republicans. To wrap it up, what this really means is that America, to quote an Islamic phrase, becomes "The Great Satan."

"It takes all the running you can do, to keep in the same place. If you want to get somewhere else, you must run at least twice as fast as that!"

The irony reaches epic proportions when one considers that one of their own, *Dr. Ben Carson*, not only ran for the presidency as a Republican, but is currently holding office in the Trump administration.

Dr. Carson did not get involved in politics because he disagrees with the SDA interpretation of Bible prophecy concerning America—at least not in regard to the points mentioned above. His views are based upon the same interpretations of Scripture and the prophetic utterances of Ellen G. White.

After deciding to join the 2016 presidential race Dr. Carson was invited to speak at the *Avondale Memorial SDA Church*, near *Sydney, Australia* on *July 12th, 2014* (*Avondale College* is one of the leading SDA institutions in that part of the world). Prior to delivering this Saturday sermon he was interviewed regarding his bid for the presidency and how this related to the prophetic views of the church. Following are some of the vital moments of that interview:

*Interviewer: I have to ask you some questions about that [Carson's bid for the presidency] because **we as Seventh-day Adventists understand the role that the United States is to play, not only** [present fulfillment of Revelation 13:11, 12] **now but in the future** ... tell me about the United States today in the whole political landscape.*

*Dr. Ben Carson: This is a country that was established for, of and by the people. It was never supposed to become for, of and by the government ... freedom of speech, freedom of religion—all of these things are **under enormous attack right now** in the United States. They have been for a while—there is an agenda. People who read a lot know exactly what I am talking about. If you go back and look at the writings of Karl Marx, Vladimir Lenin and, ah, Saul Alinsky. And they talk about how important it is to bring United States into line with everybody else in order to achieve a new world order. But in order to do that they would have to **knock down the strongest pillars, the Judeo-Christian belief system** and the strong family values. Those are the things that are under attack and that's why I am coming out so strongly against those things. And also the fact that we have to be willing to stand up for what we believe. Most Americans actually do believe in God. But **the media has been so hard on people who proclaim their faith** that most people are afraid and they've been beaten into sub-mission by the 'political correctness police.' And I have declared war on political correctness and, ah, a lot of people have joined that war ... I don't know what role the Lord has for me in all of this. **I do know when looking at prophecy that the United States will play a big role.** That there has to be a return first to a religious awakening, and, more than likely, **any persecution, particularly of the Sabbath** [Sunday law], **will come from the right, not*** *from the left* ... *people will get a little bit over- zealous and then they'll say, see how much better things are, now that we've come back to God and we need to go completely back to him, and we need to go ... you know and they're going to go overboard [pass a Sunday law and begin persecution of those who keep the 7th day Sabbath]. I hope by that time I'm not around anymore [with humour]...* [13]

"It's no use going back to yesterday, because I was a different person then"

Although Carson is a conservative, and in certain respects, might have differences of opinion with the SDA mainstream regarding political involvement and interpretation of what it means to be a nation founded on Judeo-Christian principles, it is nonetheless ironic, in light of his views concerning the United States in prophecy—providing he still is of the same opinion in 2020—that he involved himself in the Republican cause at all.

As far as the rest of the SDA leadership and membership is concerned however, it is quite another story. It is their general and often published opinion that as a church, because of what it believes, they have far more in common with Democrats than Republicans. Even though their prophetess, Ellen White, strongly spoke out against political involvement and voting for those running for political office, they now keep silent on the issue, or conveniently twist what she said and allow members to "quietly" vote and will, in how they promote the church's mission, steer the thinking of members in a direction that conforms more to a Democrat than Republican agenda.

One of the arguments used to get around Ellen White's unequivocal statements regarding voting and political involvement is to claim that, while she originally took a position against these practices, she, later in life, moved from that stance to actually encouraging people to vote.

However, in lieu of what I am addressing here, it makes little difference whether Ellen White counseled SDA's to vote or not as the entire premise for their position in regards to political involvement and voting, based on the rest of their theology, makes no sense anyway.

Indeed, what I am sharing in this book in respect to the subjects of voting and politics in the SDA "wonderland" is simply a sample of a far more complex and contradictory saga that I cover in great detail in my book *The White Elephant-In Seventh-day Adventism*. In *Chapter 16* (p. 613), titled *To Vote or Not to Vote,* I provide irrefutable evidence in support of my arguments.

For the purpose of addressing the issues I am dealing with in this work though, and in lieu of the fact that a significant portion of SDA's do go to the ballot-box to cast their vote, it might be of interest to ascertain what their leanings and logic are for voting the way they do.

"𝔜ou may have noticed that 𝔍'm not all there myself"

An SDA publication, *Spectrum Magazine* (23 October, 2014) featured a number of articles on SDA's and how and why they generally vote the way they do. One *Roundtable* article they published was titled: *I'm a*

Democrat Because of my Adventist Faith. In this article two SDA's, *Tom Gessel* and *Michael Peabody*, discuss how their SDA faith has impacted their political views. Peabody is a Republican and Gessel a Democrat, but because the majority of SDA's who vote (a fair percentage, based on Ellen G. White's statements choose not to vote at all), vote Democrat and because the reasons for this are often related to their SDA beliefs, I will focus on Gessel's contribution.

One of the very first points Gessel makes is that "Adventists who choose to align with a political party should align with the Democrats." His reason for taking this position is because, in his opinion, "Democratic policies and Adventist beliefs are relatively compatible, while Republican policies conflict with Adventist beliefs."

The first reason he gives for SDA's and Republicans not being compatible is because of Evangelical Protestants and conservative Catholics having such a powerful influence in the Republican Party. According to him, this relationship is setting the stage for something Ellen White prophesied and SDA's have been warning about for over 100 years, "the breakdown of the doctrine of separation of church and state and the consequent enactment of Sunday laws."

There is no reason, he says, to fear that "Democrats are involved in any movement that raises the threat of Sunday laws." The point he is making is that Democrats seek to establish civil laws on the basis of common sense morality and do not use "the Bible says," as a means to lend authority to that which they want to enact.

On the other hand, he contends, Republicans are "working hard to establish or repeal civil laws as necessary to oppose abortion and same-sex marriage."

And, instead of upholding their actions based solely on civil, moral concepts, they are unapologetic in upholding their actions based on what "the Bible says."

"Lose something?"

Gessel presents SDA members with a question and supplies a provocative answer. "If pro-life Adventists should not support the Republicans regarding abortion, should they support the Democrats on this issue? In my view, the answer is yes." His reason for saying "yes" to Democrats is because they do not cite God or the Bible as the authority or guide for making their choice. His answer is the same for "same-sex marriage."

His advice to SDA's is that, "under current circumstances," they "would do well to support the Democrats." To him, "Adventist support for the Republican Party makes no sense." [14]

If you are looking at America through an SDA, Ellen G. White inspired lens, then what Gessel is saying might make sense. However, if you are looking at it from a truly Biblical, Christian, historical, common-sense perspective, then, for reasons I will provide, everything he is saying makes absolutely no sense at all. Indeed, there is no doubt that he did "lose something" in "translation"—his mind.

The very first observation I will make, besides SDA's peculiar interpretation of Bible prophecy and other aspects of Scripture, is that they have a warped definition of what, in the American context—in light of origins and establishment of its unique Judeo-Christian inspired constitution—"separation of church and state" actually entails.

Separation of church and state is not really about Christians not getting involved in the affairs of the nation, by participation in the political realm or via their vote—in a nation established on Judeo-Christian principles it is absolutely unavoidable, indeed necessary, that CHRISTIANS will HAVE TO get involved.

The fact is, the very Founders of the nation, the majority of whom were Christian men—a large number of them theologians or ministers—deliberately sought to found a nation and establish a constitution based upon biblical ideals. In fact, in their deliberations, they literally studied the Bible and prayed for Divine guidance. The essence thus, of separation of church and state, is that government "separates" itself from the affairs of religious groups, in what doctrines they formulate, what they choose to believe, how they run their institutions, regardless of how weird or unscriptural those beliefs might be. The proviso however is that the practices of religious groups do not fall outside the broader parameters of the laws of the state, in that they protect the rights and safety of all citizens, regardless of their religious beliefs, or lack thereof.

So, SDA's, along with Democrats, seem to want a nation that, once its Founders had sought God to establish their Constitution on Godly, Judeo-Christian principles, would then be run in an entirely secular fashion—without God or Scripture being alluded to or consulted in respect of laws related to the morals and values that govern its citizens—notwithstanding that the very Constitution of America, in its wording, overtly references the Creator and the rights He has bestowed upon all mankind. *Benjamin Franklin* made this point so clearly when he said:

> *[I] beg I may not be understood to infer that our general Convention was Divinely inspired when it formed the new federal Constitution ... [yet]* **I can hardly conceive a transaction of such momentous importance to the welfare of millions** *now existing (and to exist in the posterity of a great nation) should be suffered to pass without being in some degree influenced,* **guided, and governed by that omnipotent, omnipresent, and beneficent Ruler in Whom all inferior spirits "live and move and have their being"** *[Acts 17:28].* [15]

If one follows the logic of SDA's and Democrats to its natural conclusion, then the argument could be: "If Americans should not consult or refer to God or 'the Bible says' when referencing an authority for formulating civil laws, then the Founders had no business bringing God into it in the first place."

In other words, why bother seeking the influence of "that omnipotent, omnipresent, and beneficent Ruler"—the Creator-God—when after all is said and done you intend to keep Him right out of it, from that time forward.

A nation founded on Godly, Judeo-Christian ideals —ostensibly a people of God—should constantly seek God, just like Israel did and was blessed for doing so, because God promised: "If my people, which are called by my name, shall humble themselves, and pray, and seek my face, and turn from their wicked ways; then will I hear from heaven, and will forgive their sin, and will heal their land" (2 Chronicles 7:14). With promises like that—especially for a nation that is going through division and turmoil—their primary goal should be to consult God's Word and seek Him for guidance.

The thing that made America unique among the nations of the world was the fact that the Founders, through Bible study and prayer, formulated the "American idea."

While doing this, surely with wisdom given from on-High, they endeavored to find the balance between being a nation founded on Judeo-Christian ideals—in other words, a nation guided by distinctly spiritual "Bible says" morals and values—yet still providing its citizens of every walk (religious or non-religious) with the freedom and liberty to choose, on the basis of conscience, how they would pursue their happiness. Freedom that would be pursued within the parameters of morals and values (laws) that were wisely and sensibly formulated and enforced so as to protect the rights and freedoms of all, especially the weak and innocent.

This approach, even though consulting God or referencing "the Bible says," does not need to entail a state-sponsored religion that enforces its agenda on all. What it simply entails, because of the very basis and origin of the entire "American experiment," is that Godly values guide the nation, because simply put, Godly values are the most sensible values anyone could ever seek to follow.

Thus, referencing God or the Bible for the source or authority behind the laws that govern the morals and values of its society, is NOT out of place—it is, indeed, unavoidable.

The founders built "protection mechanisms" into the Constitution, preventing laws from being enacted that would infringe on people's freedom to worship as they chose. Any administration that might accomplish subverting or nullifying these built in mechanisms—such as what the left has tried to do by attempting to rewrite history and denying America's Judeo-Christian origins—would immediately ensure that the very core and character of America would be forever lost.

The dilemma that SDA's and the left face is that if they should correctly interpret and accept the truth behind the establishment of the American idea, then, by default, their whole paradigm collapses and they stand completely exposed.

This is why the Democrats, especially its more hardcore leftist fringe, have been fighting for decades and decades to get God and religion out of every aspect of society. It is for this reason that SDA's would rather vote for them or not vote at all, because they are terrified of God, in any overt sense, being brought into politics, as this, in light of their prophetess, Ellen G. White's interpretation of prophecy, would mean Sunday laws and the singling out of SDA's, who will refuse to keep Sunday sacred, which will then lead to persecution, and —again, according to their interpretation of Scripture and the revelations of Ellen White—ultimately death.

It is this type of sectarian, cultic, religious fanaticism, in regard to prophecy and other unscriptural teachings that have time and time again also caused SDA leadership to resist rational and even Christian-based political ideologies and woo subversive governments or political groups, in other parts of the world, such as their courtship of Hitler and his Nazi agenda.

CHAPTER II

Eat the Magic Mushroom

SDA'S in Hitler's Wonderland

"Twinkle twinkle little bat. How I wonder
what you're at. Up and above the world you fly,
like a tea tray in the sky"

During Hitler's rise to power, during the 1930's, the largest *Protestant* group were the *Evangelicals*, which incorporated 40 million of Germany's Protestants. Included in this group were 28 regional *Landeskirchen* (regional churches) that were comprised of three major, post Reformation, theological traditions: The *Reformed*, the *United* and the *Lutheran*. There were also the "free" Protestant churches, which included *Methodists, Baptists* and also denominations such as the *SDA's*.

In the 1920's, the emergence of an Evangelically-based movement, the *German Christians*, worked to inspire its members to embrace many of the nationalistic, racially-stimulated aspects of Nazi ideology, to the extent, that when the Nazis came to power, the German Christians campaigned for the creation of a *Reich Church* (State/Empire Church). It needs to be noted that during these very early stages of

Hitler's rise, it was not readily apparent that the Nazi Party was anti-Christian.

During this phase it appeared that Hitler was willing to work with the Christian community. However, this status began to change when the darker aspects of Hitler's agenda became more apparent.

Within the Evangelical group, and in opposition to the "German Christians," emerged the *Confessing Church*, who on the basis of its founding document, the *Barmen Confession of Faith*, stated that the allegiance of the church was not to a worldly Führer, but to God. This resulted in a *Kirchenkampf* (Church struggle), which caught the attention of Hitler and led to the persecution of a number of leaders within the Confessing Church group. The most famous of these were the theologian, *Dietrich Bonhoeffer* and *Martin Niemöller*. Bonhoeffer was executed for his apparent role in trying to overthrow the regime, and *Niemöller* spent seven years behind bars for criticising Hitler.

On the whole however, even within the Confessing Church, the majority of clergy were mainly concerned with preventing the state from interfering in the affairs of the church. Within this group, there were, not only members of the clergy, but laity too, who resisted the regime and helped protect the Jews.

The *Catholic Church* was suspicious of *National Socialism* from the start and in 1933 some bishops prohibited their dioceses from affiliating with the Nazi Party. As late as 1937 a papal encyclical, *Mit brennender Sorge* (With Burning Concern)—regarding Hitler's agenda—was read from Catholic pulpits, prompting the *Gestapo* to confiscate copies from diocesan offices around the country.

Catholics, unlike the Evangelical churches, did not

experience a *Kirchenkampf* within their ranks, partly due to the activities of rabid anti-Catholic figures such as *Alfred Rosenberg*, a Nazi ideologue during the early stages of the party's rise to power. Yet, in spite of Rosenberg's activities certain prominent leaders within the Catholic Church did speak out against Hitler's agenda.

All things considered though, the general tactic, as it was with the Protestants, was an attitude of caution with respect to compromise with Nazi leadership and the level of protest they could voice without awakening the ire of the regime—"walking the fine line" between the Fuhrer and God—a compromise that never ends well.

There is little doubt, as became more apparent after 1945 and the end of World War II, that the Christian community, notwithstanding the resistance that did exist, could have done a lot more to oppose Hitler's agenda. Brave Christian leaders and laity, within Protestantism and Catholicism, risking their lives for what they believed was morally right, did speak out.

For example, in 1935, when Hitler's Aryan, anti-Jewish agenda became glaringly obvious, a protest statement was read from pulpits within the *Confessing Churches* during March of that year, resulting in the arrest of 700 pastors. However, the resistance from these faithful Christians was not enough to turn the tide.

The point that I want to make here is that, in spite of the fact that Protestants and Catholics did not do enough to resist Hitler's agenda, some, within the ranks of both these groups, were looking at the Fuhrer and asking, as the Caterpillar in Alice in Wonderland did: "Who. Are. You?"

The primary reason for the resistance that did exist was that German Christians, by and large, although they could relate to the move towards nation building, motivated by Germany's massive war-debt and the *Great Depression*, could not relate to the obvious moral dilemma that was so intrinsic to the Nazi agenda.

Where, in this milieu of Catholic, Protestant and "free" church blend, did the SDA Church stand? Were they, along with other religious leaders asking: "Who. Are. You?" Or, rather, were there significant aspects of SDA beliefs that actually contributed to facilitating a significant bond between them and Hitler's regime—the same unscriptural tendencies that bond so many of them to present-day leftist, Democrats?

Did these beliefs, from the early years of Hitler's rise, right to the close of the war, induce SDA leadership to not only actively support the Nazi Party, but also, for the sake of continued recognition and survival, cause them to remain blind and mute to the atrocities of the Third Reich?

After all, for a Church denomination who claimed, above all the other "fallen, denominational churches" on the planet, to be the only true body of faith on earth, it should have been a no-brainer what position they would take against the mechanisms of Hitler's Nazi agenda.

Sadly, this Ellen White-proclaimed "apple of God's eye," in spite of the additional Divine insight and leadership of this same prophetess, did far less than the denomination they consistently brand the anti-Christ— first beast of Revelation 13—the *Roman Catholic Church*. In fact, numerous conservative SDA evangelists make it a point to mention Nazi/Catholic collaboration in *Croatia* during *World War II* but remain strangely silent when it comes to the guilt of the SDA Church during the same period.

"𝔐𝔬𝔰𝔱 𝔢𝔳𝔢𝔯𝔶𝔬𝔫𝔢'𝔰 𝔪𝔞𝔡 𝔥𝔢𝔯𝔢"

Pastor Harold Alomia, who holds an *Mdiv* from SDA *Andrews University Seminary*, in his essay, *Fatal Flirting: The Nazi State and the Seventh-day Adventist Church*, writes:

> *Following in the footsteps of the Christian majority, **the Seventh-day Adventist Church cannot be commended for its actions during the Nazi Regime**. Echoing the praises for the rise of Hitler to power, **Adolf Minck, President of the Adventist German Church, penned his satisfaction with the election of Adolf Hitler in the August Edition of Advenbote** (the official periodical of the Seventh-day Adventist Church in Germany at that time): "**A fresh enlivening, and renewing reformation spirit is blowing through our German lands** ... this is a time of decision, a time of such opportunities for a believing youth as has not been for a long time.... **The word of God and Christianity shall be restored to a place of honor.**" Another example expressing enthusiasm for the Nazi state was **Wilhelm Mueller** who went so far as to label **Hitler as "chosen by God"** for the office of chancellor and **praising his similarity with Adventism's health reform: "As an anti-alcoholic, non-smoker, [and] a vegetarian he is closer to our own view of health reform than anybody else."**

> *Not only did the Seventh-day Adventist leadership sing praises to the Nazi government, it even went so far as **"strongly recommending" how its members were to vote** in every plebiscite of the Nazi Regime.*[16]

In fact, after the SDA Church was banned by the Nazi state in November of 1933—a ban which lasted for about ten days, till 6 December—it embarked on an even more aggressive pro-government and "Volkisch" state campaign.

No doubt, and it is an opinion held by those familiar with the history, part of the reason for the ban being lifted on the SDA Church was because of its "health reform" message, which Hitler would certainly have approved of.

It is exactly because of this common-ground on food and drink and a number of other SDA peculiarities that I will get to shortly, that ensured the SDA blind-spot remained in effect.

As far as a healthy, meat and alcohol free diet is concerned, there is certainly nothing in and of itself that is negative about that. More and more people, especially in this day and age, have opted for a vegetarian or vegan diet and there are many who choose not to drink alcohol, independent of any religious belief.

Indeed, if approached in a balanced manner, such a lifestyle is a healthy choice. However, when it comes to the SDA doctrine on things like diet, even dress and a number of other things for that matter, according to the inspired insight of Ellen G. White, it is quite another question.

"𝖂𝖍𝖞 𝖎𝖘 𝖆 𝖗𝖆𝖛𝖊𝖓 𝖑𝖎𝖐𝖊 𝖆 𝖜𝖗𝖎𝖙𝖎𝖓𝖌 𝖉𝖊𝖘𝖐?"

On the basis of the claim that God revealed these things to her, Ellen White labelled the consumption of coffee, tea, alcohol and tobacco a sin—something which God explicitly forbids. The eating of meat, or the "flesh of dead animals," as she often called it, became a question of salvation, and even, if consumed by SDA members who should know better, would "excite their animal passions," affect their "morals" and even prevent God from hearing their prayers. [17]

Her message to the leadership of the church was that if they ate "corpses," or the "flesh of dead animals" they were unfit to be messengers for the Lord. [18]

The bottom line in all of this, was that SDA health reform ended up becoming a question of salvation. In Ellen White's words: "... they are unfitted to be spiritual worshipers, and are not worthy of heaven. If man will cherish the light that God in mercy gives him upon health reform, he may be sanctified through the truth, and fitted for immortality. But if he disregards that light, and lives in violation of natural law, he must pay the penalty." [19]

Everything, from dress to the wearing of jewellery, playing in competitive sports, games of chess, cards, backgammon, all these were forbidden, because "God" had shown Ellen White that His "peculiar people," those privileged with the truth, were to be separate from the rest of the world.

For non-adventists, it is difficult to put yourself in the position of one who has membership in this "exclusive" religious "club." SDA's, especially of earlier generations, because of their foundational *sanctuary message*, which from the start turned them into the only "non-Babylonian" faith on the planet—along with all these other additional counsels, that when followed, made you worthy—contributed to their perception of their chosen status.

When it came to the question of race, which I will address more comprehensively in the segment on SDA's and *Apartheid South Africa*, there were also statements from Ellen White's "inspired pen" that helped fan the flames of prejudice.

To be fair, although she did not condone unfair treatment of non-white people, and counselled the church to labor for their souls, she did make statements that provided "inspired" evidence, for those SDA's who were more racially inclined, to treat non-white's in a way that was less than human. Indeed, Ellen White's statements on "amalgamation between man and beast," were used for justification of such. [20]

An issue closely related to the racial question was the SDA perception of Jews. Again, although Ellen White did not denigrate Jews to the trash-heap of racial ignominy, she did write strong statements about the cessation of their chosen status and the curse that they, as a people, were under because of rejecting and killing the Messiah. [21]

Just as it was with the SDA view of the world, other Christian faiths and non-Christian religions, so it was in regard to Jews who cling to their traditional Jewish beliefs—all and sundry were part of spiritual Babylon.

Of course, when every other faith in the world were relegated to such unenviable status, this assured that SDA's, at least in their minds, were the only people upon whom God bestowed His supreme regard. The remnant; the chosen; those who had been given light as no other people had been given hitherto—the primary source of THAT "light," being non other than Ellen G. White.

In spite of the fact that there is not one credible line in Scripture that supports the peculiar teachings, from the sanctuary, health reform, to questions on games, jewellery and race—unless one grossly abuses the clear testimony contained therein—the authority of Ellen White provides enough proof and fact for the faithful SDA believer.

Thus, lest it is assumed that only the SDA health

reform doctrine was a contributing factor to creating a link with Hitler, the reader can see that there were other aspects of SDA belief that attracted them to the Hitler "Volk" concept, because the entire SDA doctrine of exclusivity predisposes them to this sort of mindset. Regarding the SDA's renewed enthusiasm of the *Volk* concept, post their brief ban, Alomia writes:

> *It [SDA pro-government campaign] went on **to support the notion of the Volkisch state,** ascribing validity to that idea and saying it **was in accordance with biblical principles**. In the December 1933 edition of Gegenwartsfragen, one of the Adventist periodicals, it proudly proclaimed that **"we are part of this revolution as well— as individual Christians and also as a corporate denominational body."** [22]*

"Curiouser & Curiouser!"

On the question of Hitler's agenda concerning the Jews —SDA compromise with this no doubt legitimized by their/Ellen White's view of the Jewish "curse"—Alomia writes:

> *The acceptance of the Volk concept with **its racial undertones,** its **ideology of ethnic purity,** and its **implicit proscription of the Jews due to their racial heritage was accepted by the Seventh-day Adventist Church as part of the gospel proclamation**. A church writer stated: "The Volk when organized ... forms a Volksgemeinschaft or ethnic community, and Adventists should be among the very best members of such a community. [23]*

Alomia continues:

The adoption of this viewpoint as part of Seventh-day Adventist thought was **mixed with the church's characteristic health message** *as a means* **to court the state and to gain favor with it.** *"While continuing the traditional emphasis on healthful living, Adventist publications soon adopted elements of the Nazi racial agenda.... A curious path led from caritas, the caring for the less fortunate and weak, to* **elimination of the weak, as the work of God,** *"* [24]

As a consequence of this intensive push to validate themselves in the eyes of the Hitler regime, the SDA health message started morphing "into what the state dictated and not what Scripture taught."

Of course, as already pointed out, the SDA health message, in all its peculiar facets, cannot be substantiated by Scripture, thus, moving from one unscriptural position to an even more radically unscriptural position could be seen, when circumstances demanded such a move, as a necessary progression in order for the "remnant of the Lord" to survive, perhaps even thrive, as a religious partner of the Third Reich— the master race, together with the "master church."
Indeed, the church was well "aware of this twisting of terms and meanings" to facilitate this bond with the state. [25]

"G. W. Schubert, vice-president of the German Adventist Church, shared his 'faint hope' with a fellow *vice-President* of the *General Conference of Seventh-day Adventists* that 'perhaps this might be the way of the Lord to get the same freedom later on for the distribution of our religious literature.'" [26]

In spite of this revelation from the German SDA vice-president to the vice-president of the SDA Church's highest body of authority—the General Conference—SDA leadership did not demand an immediate halt to what was happening. All and sundry seemed quite content to go down the rabbit-hole of Hitler's Nazi agenda. After all, they had the "inspired" words of their proverbial "White Rabbit" to legitimize the entire compromise.

In fact, SDA support continued even beyond this. Alomia writes that "the Adventist Church also agreed with the forced sterilization policy, also known as the Eugenics Laws.… Again, hermeneutical acrobatics were used to defend the government's position ... The farfetched explanation suggested the notion that Christians should 'not [be] interfering with nature's process of cleansing the nation's racial pool.'" [27]

This process, however, would not stop at forced sterilization but would quickly progress to elimination (euthanasia) of those who would "infect" the German gene pool. SDA's, in order to avoid another banishment shut their mouths and went along with the agenda. Alomia records that *Ronald Blaich*, author of *The Case for the Seventh-day Adventist Church,* describes the situation stating "... that German Adventist leaders eagerly courted Nazi goodwill by accommodating to the new order." [28]

Interestingly the church-groups that vocally opposed the Nazi euthanasia agenda, in the face of SDA silence, were *Catholics* and *Lutherans*. Irony cannot even begin to describe this debacle—the end-time, satanically inspired first beast of Revelation 13 (according to SDA's, the Papal Church), condemning the murder of innocent people, while the "the bride of Christ," His chosen people (SDA's), the one's "who have the truth," born in the U.S.A., land of the free and the brave (according to them, the second satanically inspired beast of that same chapter), become enthusiastic supporters of arguably the most evil, fascist empire the world has ever seen.

Sadly, what happened in Germany during the rule of Hitler's regime, was not just some crazy exception. This type of racially inspired compromise continued in South Africa before and during the rule of the apartheid government.

In fact, it is this same kind of SDA blind-spot, because of unscriptural, Ellen White inspired teachings, that so many members have accepted hook, line and sinker, that ensure SDA alignment with the leftist, Democrat agenda in the present. Unless there is a radical change, this will continue to be their Achilles-heel into the future.

CHAPTER III

Simply Impassable

Seventh-day Adventists
& Apartheid South Africa

"Come, come now. Crying won't help"

The question of racial discrimination in South Africa is not something that only became an issue in the early 1960's, when South Africa officially gained independence and became a Republic. Separation along lines of color, in all spheres of life, existed from the very start. However, formal "Apartheid" policies that were enacted by the *National Party*, when it was elected to power in 1948, under leadership of *D. F. Malan*, introduced an official change. This change would build to intense internal conflict, lead to criticism and pressure from the international community and crippling sanctions, before the official end of the Apartheid Government in 1994.

For the SDA Church in South Africa, separation along the color line was nothing new. From its conception, the South African SDA community entertained racial bias. Wealthy diamond magnate, and early SDA convert, *Philip Wessels*, who's family donated large sums of money to the SDA cause in America, Australia and South Africa, wrote to *Ellen G.*

White on 14 January 1893, expressing his ideas on the question of race within the church:

> *I do not want my children to associate with the lower classes of coloured people. I will labor for them and teach my children to do so. But I do not want my children to mix with them for such is detrimental to their moral welfare. Nor do I want my children to think there is no difference in society that they should finally associate and marry into coloured blood.... So there is the colour line drawn which is very distinctly drawn here in society. For my part I do not care. I can shake hands with the coloured people and so forth. But our association with them is going to spoil our influence with others who are accustomed to these things ... to have any influence with the higher class of people, we must respect these differences.* [29]

As far as the SDA denomination in South Africa was concerned, this attitude of segregation between whites and non-whites was not simply a question of personal preference. From early on racial segregation became part of the official SDA modus-operandi.

Jeff Crocombe, senior lecturer of Theology, at SDA *Helderberg College*, in South Africa, points out, "the Adventist church was always far ahead of the government of the day in applying racial segregation in the church, and far behind when it comes to scrapping racially discriminatory measures. By the time apartheid was introduced in law after 1948, Adventists had been practicing it for twenty or more years." [30]

In 1971, when black Zimbabwean student *Robert Hall* was "grudgingly permitted to enrol at Helderberg College.... He was not permitted to board in the dormitory, nor to eat in the cafeteria; nor was he allowed to graduate with his class.... That same year, the administration of Helderberg College asked the South African Government 'to rule on the acceptance of a foreign non-white at an all-white South African educational institution.'" The government replied that "it was not, and never had been, government policy to interfere in the training of ministers by any denomination." [31] Thus, the practice of barring non-white students from the institution had not been because of laws of the state but because of the racist bias of the SDA institution itself.

It must be noted that right from the start, going back to the founding of the SDA Church in South Africa and the communications between Wessels and Ellen White, right up until 1985, the *General Conference*, the leading authority of the SDA Church, located in *Washington D.C., U.S.A.*, did practically nothing to address the racial issues in the South African SDA community.

Even though, in 1981, a "General Conference *Commission on Church Unity* was formed to investigate the issue of race relations in South Africa," the whole affair essentially came to nothing. In spite of the fact that the commission spent 13 days conducting interviews and meetings, It spent "only four hours of its entire time in South Africa with the victims of apartheid, the Africans." [32]

In fact, after the apartheid system was dismantled and a demand for recognition of racist practices in the South African SDA church was requested, SDA leadership, instead of offering a definitive statement regarding their personal choice in the matter, attempted to put the blame elsewhere.

While they did apologize, stating, "We are deeply

sorry and plead for the forgiveness of God and our fellow citizens," [33] they excused themselves by saying that "The Seventh-day Adventist church community was a victim of the governmental system...." [34] As has already been pointed out, this blame shifting was a total misrepresentation of the facts.

What will never be said by SDA's themselves is that justification for the church's racist attitudes in South Africa and elsewhere in the world, including America, was based on certain inspired statements by prophetess Ellen G. White. Of course, I know this to be a fact because I was born and raised as an SDA, educated at Helderberg College during the apartheid years, and starting in my mid 30's, actively ministered in the SDA Church in South Africa during the dismantling of the apartheid system. Hence, I am very familiar with the use of Ellen White's statements in defense of racial or segregationist attitudes within the church.

I might add that I sat as a delegate in numerous meetings where the question of unification was discussed and where votes were taken and am personally familiar with the leadership—some were friends—and attitudes that were expressed during the entire process.

"Careful, she's stark raving mad!"

In regards to Ellen G. White's commentary on the subject of race, there is one particular statement that I heard people quote numerous times, in order to make the point that blacks were inferior to whites. This particular quote, although not directly addressing the question of separate development, had a definite effect on how they approached the question of "apartheid" between blacks and whites. Regarding the genetic blending of "man and beast," before and after the flood, Ellen White wrote:

> *Every species of animals which God had created was preserved in the ark. The confused species which God did not create, which were **the result of amalgamation**, were destroyed by the flood. Since the flood, there has been **amalgamation of man and beast**, as may be seen in the almost endless varieties of species of animals, and in **certain races of men.*** [35]

Before I comment on the actual content of the statement, let me assure the reader that SDA church historians and scholars have written many articles on the subject of this Ellen White statement, in order to defend her and refute those who claim that she was not actually stating what she so plainly did state.

In my book, *The White Elephant—In Seventh-day Adventism*, I address this question in great detail and clearly show, based on the historical evidence—using Ellen White's own words and those of her husband *James White,* in conjunction with other church leaders of the day—proving that she was talking about amalgamation (hybridization or the blending of genes) between animals and black people from Africa. [36]

Indeed, Uriah Smith, An SDA Church leader during the time of Ellen White, authored the book, *The Visions of Mrs. E. G. White, A Manifestation of Spiritual gifts According to the Scripture*—the book was endorsed and promoted by the White's—in which he explains her statement as meaning, that although the effects of amalgamation could still be seen in certain species of men, this did not mean that they were not human and then went on to mention some of the races in which these effects could still be seen.

> *... they [those who doubt Ellen White's vision on amalgamation] could easily be silenced by a reference to such cases as the **wild Bushmen of Africa**, some tribes of the **Hottentots** [in South Africa], and perhaps the **Digger Indians** of our own country[America], &c. Moreover, **naturalists affirm that the line of demarcation between the human and animal races is lost in confusion**. It is **impossible**, as they affirm, **to tell just where the human ends and the animal begins**.* [37]

Thus, on the basis of this "inspired" evidence, SDA's in South Africa, in Nazi Germany and elsewhere in the world, felt justified, at least to some "reasonable" extent, to view black people as inferior to whites.

As it is with everything the SDA Church does, in order to defend itself and its prophetess, a lot of exegetical tap-dancing, sanitizing of Ellen White statements and twisting of the facts takes place, in order to make her plainer and more embarrassing statements less objectionable.

Indeed, apologists for Ellen White have practically developed an art-form out of taking her more contradictory statements and creating what they call "balance" and "progression" of divine insight and thought. Yet, what these kinds of statements more often than not are, are the consequence of her attempting to correct her "inspired revelations," that were coming back to bite her, without making the contradictions glaringly obvious.

On the basis of those who knew the White's personally and who shared with others what they had heard, it can easily be understood why SDA brethren in South Africa and elsewhere, interpreted Ellen White the way they did. A knowledge of Ellen White's personal and inspired views—after all, she was the supreme, spiritual guide of the entire denomination—lent legitimacy to their treatment of colored people.

A prime example of leading brethren who knew James and Ellen White personally and who were privy to some of the racial views held by them, were *Elders B.F. Snook* and *W.H. Brinkerhoff*. James had made Ellen's view known to *Elder Ingraham* who then passed it on to Snook and Brinkerhoff. They later wrote about the "amalgamation" visions and what they had heard from Snook, concluding:

> *Here is what she [Ellen White] says; "Since the flood there has been amalgamation of man and beast, as may be seen in the almost endless varieties of species, and in certain races of men"…. But what are we to understand by certain races of men? She has not informed us in her writings, but left us to fix the stigma of amalgamation where we may see fit. But the interpretation has come to light. She told it to her husband, and he made it known to Eld. Ingraham, and he divulged the secret to the writer, that **Sister White had seen that God never made the Darkey** [colored people].* [38]

Although Ellen White's inspired statements on amalgamation of man and beast and the origins of black people did embolden the brethren in South Africa to view black people as "not entirely human," it was her direct testimonies regarding church operations that provided the authority to officially put their separatist agenda into practice, such as her counsel to "let white and colored people be labored for in separate, distinct lines." [39]

Ellen White wrote, in regard to leadership of the work in America—a principle that was applied in South Africa and elsewhere—that "white men must be chosen as leaders." [40] In fact, in addition to this she counseled that "... Colored People should not urge that they be placed on an equality with White People," [41] and that the "... work of proclaiming the truth for this time is not to be hindered by an effort to adjust the position of the Negro race." [42]

She counseled against marriage between white and black people, because "... all should consider that they have no right to entail upon their offspring that which will place them at a disadvantage ... there should be no intermarriage between the white and the colored race." [43]

None of the brethren questioned the authority behind these counsels because Ellen White said that "the light given me of the Lord was that this step [marriage between white's and colored's] should not be taken." [44]

Thus, if anyone had an issue with this position, it would be a question of being at odds with the authority of God and not mere human opinion.

On January 8, 1901, she wrote to a young man who was planning to marry a colored girl, counseling:

> *Do not unite yourself in marriage with a girl who will have cause to regret the step forever after.... O what covetous, selfish, short-sighted creatures human beings are. Distrust your own judgment, and depend on the judgment of God. Distinguish between what is pleasing and what is profitable.* [45]

Notwithstanding the evidence presented, it needs to be said that Ellen White did encourage the church to evangelise among the colored people and grant them membership in the church. [46]

However, her counsel regarding separation, expectations that colored people should have and who should be in charge of the work, together with her statements about amalgamation and her obvious racial bias, most certainly had an effect on—not only the patronizing attitude of white's towards blacks in South Africa and America—but also contributed to the feelings of European superiority in Hitler's Nazi Germany.

As I pointed out earlier on, for SDA's, this perception of superiority was not only about racial elitism but also about spiritual or denominational superiority. As claimed by *SDA General Conference President, Ted Wilson, Revelation 12:17* describes "God's remnant people who 'keep the commandments of God, and have the testimony of Jesus,'" as "constituted in ONLY one body of faith today: the Seventh-day Adventist Church." [47]

CHAPTER IV

Everything's got a Moral if Only You can Find It

"If you don't think, you shouldn't talk!"

It is an interesting fact that those Christian denominations in the United States of America that have some sort of prejudice towards government, that do not vote or get involved in politics, that have reservations about the military, or vote predominantly Democrat, have common origins. The most well known of these are *SDA's, Jehovah's Witnesses* and the *Church of God (7th Day)*. All three of these have their origins in the post *Millerite Adventist,* 1844 disappointment era. In fact, *Charles Russel,* founder of the Jehovah's Witnesses, was strongly influenced by the post 1844 Adventist message.

The founders of the Church of God (7th Day), which today has a number of breakaway groups, were at one time brethren of influence in the fledgling SDA Church, who finally left because, among other things, they believed Ellen White to be a false prophet. [48]

Among these three denominations, SDA's have the largest membership. *Worldwide* SDA membership is presently in excess of *18 million,* and in *North America,* over *1 million.* One can only imagine, taking into account the combined membership of these three major denominations—SDA's, Jehovah's Witnesses and the Church of God (7th Day)—what impact their peculiar teachings have on their membership in relation to government, and particularly, in the case of SDA's, what effect their view of America in prophecy impacts on how they will either vote, or as the case may be, not vote at all.

Evangelicals (some view SDA's as Evangelical, which they definitely are not), *Roman Catholics, Mormons* and a number of other Protestant groups, that are actively involved in the political arena and regularly vote, are on the whole conservative in their views and lean Republican in their party affiliation. Additionally, especially in the case of Evangelicals, they uphold the Constitution, embrace the nation's Judeo-Christian origins, believe in the idea of American exceptionalism, are Bible-based in their ideas on morals and values, and in lieu of the nations Christian roots, encourage government to uphold moral standards that compliment those origins.

This is not about attempting to turn government into a religious institution, an endeavour to establish a state religion, or force everyone, irrespective of their spiritual beliefs, or lack thereof, to accept by law, a Christian-based moral code. Rather, what it is about is ensuring that a nation of Judeo-Christian origins, founded and established by Christians, uses as the blueprint for its morals and values, the best code for human morality and conduct that the universe has at its disposal—the standard of the Creator—God Himself.

Indeed, even the Creator, having given man the perfect code for morals and values, permits the freedom to choose whether or not to obey that code—natural consequence notwithstanding. Which means that there are certain things in regard to an individual's moral choice, when it does not endanger the rights of other free moral-agents or the innocent and helpless, that government cannot and should not legislate—for or against.

However, any Christian who would want to waive high moral standards that are appropriately legislated for governing society, in order to avoid association with "the Bible says," while yet professing Christianity, is speaking out of both sides of their mouth.

Unfortunately, in the case of SDA's, there is a tremendous double-standard when it comes to their professed conservative values and what they expect from those who legislate the laws of the land. As revealed earlier, SDA's who vote Democrat, have no problem— should Democrats get their way—legislating abortion on demand. They are also content with legislating gay marriage and other practices connected to L.G.B.T.Q. community demands, in spite of the fact that a government should have no business legislating for or against consensual, adult gay relationships. When it comes to the moral question of protecting the lives of helpless, defenseless, innocent unborn babies however, it is an entirely different story. In this case, government has a duty to enact appropriate laws that forbid and punish such practices.

On the subject of abortion, there can be no greater

hypocrisy than that which is publicly revealed, as opposed to what is more covertly practiced in SDA medical institutions. Those who are familiar with some of the morally conservative teachings of the SDA Church and their humanitarian endeavors around the world, might imagine they would be wholly on the pro-life side; however, this is not even vaguely the case.

Practice in SDA medical institutions that offer abortion are almost entirely pro-choice/abortion on demand, something which most SDA members are largely ignorant of. There are even cases where babies, once outside the womb—alive and crying—have been suffocated to death. For example, one shocked pediatrician recounted her experience working in an Adventist hospital to *Richard Fredericks, Ph.D.*, who writes:

> *...* ***The baby was born alive and crying, but placed in a sealed bucket to suffocate****. She [the pediatrician] was horrified by such **an act of murder**. Beyond the initial horror she was **stunned on two accounts**: first, **during her own training she had stated she would withdraw from medical school** (University of Virginia) **rather than perform or participate in an abortion due to her religious convictions** as an Adventist. After first saying she must assist in an abortion to graduate, the University backed down. She **assumed as a church we took a strong stand against abortion.** Then she found that **abortions for convenience** (non-medical emergencies) **were regular occurrences in Adventist hospitals**. I will never forget her tears as she looked at me and said: "How can we do this?"* [49]

This lack of conscience in regard to these practices in SDA medical institutions, can in fact, be attributed to their doctrinal belief concerning the commencement of a viable life-form, which incidentally, is why they found it so easy to go along with Hitler's forced sterilization policy/Eugenics Laws. In an article published by *Proclamation Magazine*, *Colleen Tinker* described it thus:

> *The hidden history and practice of abortion within the Adventist organization is **the fruit of a religion that believes and teaches a false view of humanity** on one hand while offering medical care on the other to some of the most vulnerable members of society: women with unwanted pregnancies. Because **they believe human fetuses are unviable forms of life until they can survive outside the womb**, many Adventist doctors offer their patients the option of abortions as a "compassionate" way to resolve their dilemmas.* [50]

If SDA's believe, as most Christians with a moral compass do, that a baby in the womb is a living child that experiences emotion and reacts to various stimuli from the outside world—e.g., they have a profound sensitivity to music and tones of the human voice—then they should be filled with terror when recalling Christ's dire warning to those who would dare harm a little child. It would be better for such a one, He said, "that a millstone be hanged about his neck, and that he were drowned in the depths of the sea" (Matthew 18:6).

To be sure, the majority of SDA members—even those who might lean towards the liberal left—are more than likely pro-life. However, because of the nature of the SDA "beast" and the tendency of its leadership to justify compromise and contradiction, under "inspired" instruction of the schizoid teachings of Ellen G. White, the grossest of practices have been, not only tolerated, but encouraged; the afore-examined issues of abortion, racism and Nazi genocide being prime examples.

This practice of talking out of both sides of one's mouth, and, under the direction of a false prophet, making it up as you go along, was happening from the very birth of the SDA Church denomination—in relation to government, politics, military and a slew of other issues. The positions taken by Ellen G. White and the SDA brethren regarding the question of voting and involvement in politics being a primary case-in-point.

CHAPTER V

That's Logic!

*"Well, I can't put it any more clearly, sir,
for it isn't clear to me."*

On the basis of what I have shared throughout this book, in regards to SDA's in *Nazi Germany*, the question of *race* and *Apartheid South Africa*, their position and activity in connection to *abortion*, their belief concerning *America* and their *attitude to politics*, it is easy to see how they, unlike genuine Evangelicals, find it so convenient to align themselves with leftist Democrats, rather than conservative Republicans—barring some exceptions, such as Dr. Carson and some others that seem to have a more informed view of the world around them.

On the one hand, ironically so, the SDA denomination was born in a land that offered liberty to its citizens and the freedom to pursue the religion of their choice, yet—under the protection of those privileges—has been able to indoctrinate and subvert its members into believing that they, SDA's, are the ONLY true faith on earth and that the land which offered them the freedom to style themselves as such, is the satanically inspired beast of the apocalypse.

This suits the SDA institution because its whole system is really the antithesis of freedom. For them, all the rest of the world—religious and political—are apostate and fallen.

When it comes to the final countdown for planet earth, eternal freedom and salvation for anyone only exists within the parameters of SDA exclusivism and conformity to its oppressive, singular salvational philosophy and unscriptural beliefs.

On the other hand, American Democrats, born in that same land, have also used and abused those same freedoms to further their political agenda. For them, the American way (freedom of expression) has provided a free ride for indoctrinating and subverting generations of Americans, via education, the media and every other means at their disposal, into believing a false narrative of American history, rejecting the idea of American exceptionalism and the nation's Judeo-Christian origins.

In just about every respect, albeit that one is secular and the other religious, they are the consummate twins, the proverbial yin and yang, thesis and anti-thesis—the Hegelian dialectic in action. Two pretenders in tandem on a bicycle made for two, who are peddling the lie that they, politically and spiritually, are the answer to everything that is wrong with the nation of America, and for that matter, the rest of the world.

It is the abuse of liberty and freedom, in religious and secular realms, indispensable and necessary though they might be, that also style them a two-edged sword— in a fallen world, their strength is also their inherent weakness. This is unavoidable, and in fact what God has permitted, so that all humans, when exercising their freedom of choice, choose either good or evil—the choice is, rightfully, theirs to make. However, the other side of that double-edged sword is that religious or political institutions can, and indeed do, when motivated by anything other than the purest of motives, abuse that freedom.

Ironically, whether they consciously intend it or not, SDA's and the political left are aiding and abetting each other to realize their respective goals.

SDA's, or any other faith for that matter that claim to be God's one "true" church or "remnant," invariably feel threatened by a political entity that operates on the basis of Judeo-Christian ideals, especially if some of those ideals contradict the teachings of their "superior" SDA faith.

For SDA's, based on their warped idea of what "separation of church and state" actually means, it might be better to have a government that is entirely secular than one that is run by Christian politicians who happen to be members of Catholicism or any of the other "fallen denominational churches" (Babylon)—so labeled by Ellen G. White.

This is why, whether in Nazi Germany, apartheid South Africa or America—where leftist-democrats are leaning more and more towards pure socialism and moving ever further from those morals and values upon which the American nation was founded—SDA's do a balancing act between infidelity and true Christianity, creating their own unique synthesis of right and wrong in order to survive and continue as the self-proclaimed apple of God's eye (His true remnant church). Indeed, when it comes to most things in the "wonderland" of Seventh-day Adventism, very little seems to actually make sense at all.

**"Nothing would be what it is because everything
would be what it isn't. And contrariwise, what it is,
it wouldn't be, and what it wouldn't be,
it would. You see?"**

In order to expand and nail down a number of issues I addressed earlier I would like to draw your attention to an official SDA publication. The November/December 2019 issue of SDA *Liberty* magazine, published a number of articles that clearly demonstrate the church's inability to have a balanced perspective on the relationship between church and state and religious freedom in a nation that is guided by a Constitution that was intentionally framed upon Judeo-Christian morals and values.

One article, written by *Asma T. Udin,* author of the recent book, *When Islam Is Not A Religion. Inside America's Fight for Religious Freedom,* discusses the inconsistency of fundamentalist, right-wing Americans who are singling out the Muslim faith—on the basis of the teachings of Sharia law—declaring that "Islam is not a religion" but rather a political ideology. Hence, it is concluded, Islam does not have the right to enjoy the freedoms extended to other religions in America.

Asma, while quoting the first sentence of the *First Amendment*, which states that "Congress shall make no law respecting the establishment of religion, or prohibiting the free exercise thereof ...," seems to ignore the fact that freedom of religious exercise must be subject to those rights which bespeak every citizens right to "life," "liberty," "freedom" and the "pursuit of happiness."

Thus, if the exercise of your religious "rights" or "freedoms" infringe on the general life, liberty, freedom and happiness of other citizens, then your religious practice directly opposes an intrinsic RIGHT that the "Creator" extended to the entire human race—a right enshrined in America's Bill of Rights.

This is why, even though, e.g., a Satanist might have the right to practice his "faith," he does NOT have the right to participate in human sacrifice—because he then negates someone else's God-given rights.

Does Islam, regardless of whether every believer participates in such practice—on an official and even national level—negate these basic human rights? It's a no-brainer, the answer is, emphatically, yes! Yes, because there are entire nations that practice and enforce a system of Islamic religio-political government—where the laws of state and religious practice are entirely inseparable. Where some of the most reprehensible practices of Sharia law are part of daily life.

Asma ignores these facts and goes on to declare:

When people try to carve out exceptions to religious freedom, they also inevitably cede power to the government to regulate beliefs it does not like—and while Islam may be the disfavoured religion in America today, tomorrow that religion might be yours. [51]

If your "religious freedom" allows you to invalidate the basic rights of others then you need to recognise that you are actually confused about what the whole idea of "freedom" is.

The American Constitution was formulated by Christian men, some of whom were preachers and Bible scholars, who intentionally set about establishing a nation that had broken away from the oppression of religious tyranny—tyranny that was practiced under the banner of Christianity—exercised by rulers, popes and monarchs who were operating religio-political dictatorships, where religion and the laws of state had become so meshed that their subjects were persecuted for not practicing their faith in accordance with the dictates of government.

If Islamic immigrants are inspired by the same motivations as were the Pilgrims who came to America —who were fleeing religio-political oppression so they could practice TRUE Christianity—then they would not try to defend a religion that is literally negating freedom for entire nation's of people in the Middle and Far East. They would—and I am sure that many do—come to America with the same desire to break free from repressive religio-politcal Islam and declare, along with those Pilgrims who fled religio-political Christian oppression in the Old World centuries ago, that the American way guarantees freedom within parameters of Divinely instituted rights that are extended to every human being, regardless of religious belief. These are beliefs that can and should never be negated.

Indeed, Islam, whether as a whole or via its more extreme militant elements, does not only force its faith on those millions of citizens who are subjects in countries under its rule, but often, under pretense and dishonestly diabolical means, comes to America and the rest of the free world to kill those who do not choose to follow the doctrines of the prophet Muhammed. Literally thousands, in America alone, have been murdered by the jihadic sword of global Islamic inquisitors.

Should anyone of any faith, whether Islam, Hindu or Christian, expect American citizens to pretend that the activities of murderers who are carrying out heinous crimes under the auspices of their faith, have nothing to do with their religious beliefs?

The only way that a country who is trying to protect the rights and freedoms of its citizens can deal with such a dangerous situation is to investigate the actual religion that is the proclaimed inspiration behind that which is being perpetrated against innocent peace-loving Americans.

After all, some of the most prominent leaders of Islamic faith, such as the Ayatollah's in Iran, are inspiring their believers to chant "Death to America!" What else can a country do but examine the inspiration behind the crimes?

One has to be practically brain-dead to imagine that a government, who's duty it is to protect its citizens, would not examine every aspect—whether religious or political—of what might be inspiring terrorists to come across the ocean to brutally murder as many innocent people as they can.

Instead of recognizing this, SDA *Liberty* magazine publishes an article that suggests that America is denying its own ideals of separation of church and state and freedom of religion by being wary of and investigating a religion who's adherents have already been guilty of slaughtering thousands of unsuspecting human beings and who still, literally, enforce Sharia law and practice in those countries under their control.

My question to the SDA General Conference and leadership is: "where the heck were you when Hitler was slaughtering millions of Jews in Europe during World War II? Where in tarnation were you when apartheid South Africa was putting into practice its racist agenda?"

As a 4th generation SDA, who grew up in apartheid South Africa and who has investigated everything that

SDA's, under guidance of their prophetess Ellen White, have done, I can say without hesitation (together with those who are reading this book): "I know where you were ... you were walking the fine line between blind faith and true religion ... the teachings of Christ and the rantings of your false, deluded prophetess, Ellen G. White." No wonder you find yourselves imagining that America, by questioning Islam and protecting the freedoms of its peace-loving, law-abiding citizens—rights enshrined in the very doctrines of its Constitution—is denying freedom of religion and separation of church and state in regard to Islam.

Because, the truth be told, you do not even know what it means. Because of spiritual arrogance and the words of your false prophetess, you believe that you, SDA's, "God's only true church," will be the next item on the menu of religious persecution in America.

The irony of *Liberty* magazine continues in another article entitled *Life and Glory, The Vital Portion of the Declaration of Independence*—a republication of a July 1902 article by editor *John D. Bradley*, taken from *The Sentinel of Christian Liberty*.

In this article Bradley, in respect to the portion of the *Declaration of Independence* that says: "all men are created equal; that they are endowed by their Creator with certain unalienable rights ... life, liberty, and the pursuit of happiness," rightfully states:

> *Take from the Declaration those few sentences which go back of all governments and all human institutions, which grasp the throne of the infinite by holding up as immutable and inalienable the rights which exist by virtue of the existence of God and His creatures—take from the Declaration these sentences, and its life and glory are gone. Then it becomes indeed what the great Lincoln*

declared it would be when thus emasculated: "Mere rubbish—old wadding left to rot on the battlefield after the victory is won." [52]

Bradley is certainly right, but the SDA interpretation of his sentiments—based on their understanding of life, liberty and the pursuit of happiness, in religious and civil context—is not.

In fact, the SDA conundrum manifests itself rather starkly in an article entitled, *Natural Laws, The Abortion Debate Turns Legislative*. The article, written by *Ed Cook,* who holds a doctorate in church-state studies, adequately demonstrates how "out on a limb" the SDA denomination is regarding the question of religion, personal choice and those intrinsic rights of "life, liberty, and the pursuit of happiness."

The essential point that Cook is trying to make, by using the example of the November 2019 vote of 59 % of Alabama State voters to recognize the rights of the unborn, is that religious convictions that motivate political decisions are not acceptable and are thus contrary to the spirit of the Constitution (all 25 Senators who voted to support the bill—some motivated by religious conviction—were Republicans and all 6 who voted against are Democrats). In response to those who voted on the grounds of religious beliefs, and in an attempt to paint such motives as illegitimate, Cook, in conjunction with quoting the *New York Times*, writes:

... exploring the religious motive further, the New York Times published an article on May 16, 2019. "In Alabama opposition to abortion runs deep," in which reporters revealed through interviews of many Alabamians that indeed religion was among primary

motives to amend the states constitution to favour the rights of the unborn, as well as to pass the new law banning abortions. [53]

Cook goes on to say:

> *... in Alabama there is a distinct difference between merely being anti-abortion and pro-life.*
>
> *History shows that combining religion and politics results in losses for both. Religion that co-opts the political process becomes a persecuting force. In such circumstances religion loses its divine character and becomes sullied with the carnal nature of contenders in the ring of power politics.*
>
> *... Politicians who co-opt religion utilize such a ploy to appease religionists, but in turn dissociate themselves from the non-religious segment of society, resulting in further division within an already fragmented populace.* [54]

Cook has more to say, but the bottom line is that his diatribe leads to one inevitable conclusion—SDA's are indeed very confused and contradictory in their understanding regarding religion and politics in a nation that was established on morals and values of Judeo-Christian origin.

If one is going to approach the question of politicians making decisions on the grounds of religious conviction, in the way that Cook and SDA's do, then you might as well declare, as Lincoln so rightly stated concerning the Declaration (quoted by Liberty magazine, to support their argument in a previous article) that it might as well be relegated: "Mere rubbish—old wadding left to rot on the battlefield after the victory is won."

As pointed out earlier, the *Declaration of Independence*, the *Bill of Rights*, indeed the *Constitution* of the United States was established by Christian politicians, many of whom were preachers and Bible scholars, by intentionally and very categorically referencing the Bible —the Divine source for their moral convictions and enactments. That is why they spoke of the "Creator," God, who bestowed upon mankind certain "unalienable rights."

This is why, even today, Presidents, while putting their hand on the Bible, are sworn into office and then declare: "so help me God." This is why you can read in crisp, clear letters on the wall of the House Chamber and American bank notes: "In God We Trust." Simply put, the Founders/politicians of the day, referenced their religious morals and convictions to establish the very documents upon which the American nation was founded!

There should be NO embarrassment, NO fear of turning off non-believers, NO inherent negative side to testifying that your belief in the morals and values of the eternal, Divine Constitution (God's Standards), are what inspire you to vote the way you choose!

Skeptics might accuse these people of using their religiously inspired vote as a "ploy," but that is all it remains, an accusation, because they cannot read the heart. Yet, even if some dishonest politicians are using Christian faith as a "ploy," the fact still remains that if religious conviction was good enough for those Founders of the American nation, then a faith-based motivation for choosing right over wrong should be good enough for both politicians and citizens in this age too—particularly when going to cast their vote!

Surely, everyone knows, even Christian

denominations and other religious establishments are filled with no less compromise, dishonesty, sin, power-grabbing, self-preservation and hidden agendas than political institutions. What I have revealed in this book, using the SDA denomination, its history and current philosophy as my prime example, should adequately settle that reality. Indeed, what I have revealed here is not even the half of it.

Something such as abortion—the murder of living, helpless, innocent babies—should never be viewed as a question of "personal choice." Being "pro-life" is about the nation and its laws protecting every human-being's "unalienable right to life, liberty and the pursuit of happiness"—especially when they are unable to defend themselves.

Political correctness in regard to murder—in order to avoid courting favour with Christians or to avoid offending non-Christians—should not, even vaguely, be a consideration.

When people in power are flagrantly sacrificing eternal morals and values on the alter of doing that which God expressly condemns and finds repugnant, then Christians, whether common citizens or political leaders, should use it as an opportunity to unite and witness to the morals and values of the One true God of the Universe.

Just like *Shadrach, Meshach* a n d *Abednego* (political advisors in the Babylonian court), refused to bow down to Nebuchadnezzar's golden statue on the Plain of Dura—in front of thousands of offended pagans and their king—or like *Daniel,* a political advisor to *King Darius*, who was prepared to rather go to the lion's den than act ashamed of praying to and testifying about his God, that is how Christians should be today.

Blind Faith   BRIAN S. NEUMANN

As I pointed out before, it is exactly because of the fear of standing for right, that caused SDA's to find common-ground with Hitler and support his eugenics plan and shut their mouth's to the murder of millions. It was this same attitude that caused them to not only support but participate in the racism of the South African apartheid regime and that now—clearly demonstrating that they have still not learned their lesson—causes them to shut their mouths and rather opt for defending the "rights" of leftist-democrats who promote the murder of helpless, living, innocent babies. Whether by SDA's or any other religious body, there is only one word to describe such blatant cowardice, compromise and courtship of evil … "disgusting!"

Conclusion

On the one hand—in the name of all that is true, just and sane—indignation tempts me to go on a lengthy tirade and cry out to SDA's: "What is wrong with you? Have you forgotten that it was Catholics and other Christians —that your prophetess calls the 'fallen denominational churches/Babylon'—that spoke out against the practices of Hitler's Nazi regime, while you shut your mouths and actually co-opted to find common-ground and support his murderous agenda? Was that true spiritual insight or just blind faith?"

I feel this same urge when it comes to the political left—not just in America but around the world—to question the source and motive for their morals and values: "Is it a case of blind faith in a political ideology that has, over and over again, been proven to be defective? Is it stupidity? Is it—maybe this is closer to the truth—power, greed and a desire for absolute control?"

However, before I single out SDA's and Democrats and get carried away with denouncing the many inconsistencies that characterise their causes—which have already been amply exposed in this book—I need to remind myself and my readers that the buck of moral compromise and blind faith does not stop at the door of SDA's and the political left. Every sinful, fallen human being—in an individual or collective sense—are prone to these same maladies. Myself included.

It is a natural desire for people to want to believe that they are part of a group or cause that have it all worked out, that are special and unique, that have a knowledge or insight into spiritual truth, political solutions—or whatever other philosophy it might be— that are superior.

It is not just the SDA denomination—in the religious sphere—or the leftist Democrats in the American political arena, that are prone to elitism and moral compromise. Indeed, most assuredly, it is not only the SDA church with its cultic tendencies and faith in the unscriptural teachings of a fallible prophetess, that have sometimes caused it, in the name of self-preservation, blind faith and spiritual pride, to support and even participate in that which is patently godless and morally corrupt.

All forms of exclusivity in religion tend to lead people into developing attitudes of superiority. For example, *Islam,* believe that they are the only true worshippers of *Allah* (God) and that America and the rest of the world—religiously or in respect to political ideology—are part of the greater "Satan." Within their already exclusive religious ideology, they, internally, breed fanatical sects and cults—*Isis* being a prime example. These tendencies are especially apparent in faith movements that establish themselves on the teachings of some extra-biblical authority who claim that they have been privy to special insight that no one else has received—that God personally chose them to be the human conduit for revealing these truths to the rest of the world.

On a smaller scale, there are the *Jim Jones'* of this world who con people into drinking their spiritual "cool-aid," and people like *David Koresh* (whose teachings were an adaptation and offshoot of Ellen G. White, SDA origin), who attracted many extreme elements from within the SDA faith to join his exclusive cause and sacrifice themselves for his version of "truth."

On a larger scale, besides Islam or the SDA faith, institutions, such as the *Papacy*, conducted inquisitions and religious crusades to root out all and sundry who dared question their claim of religious pre-eminence or Papal infallibility.

In fact, throughout the history of Christianity, the moment a spiritual awakening starts to claim special insight or exclusive status, it immediately shifts from being a "witness" to God and Scripture to becoming—on the strength of a singular individual's so-called inspired revelations—the "one" avenue through which salvation can be obtained.

As already alluded to earlier, America itself has been the birthplace for a number of religious movements who claimed that they alone were the ones who had the "truth" (Jehovah's Witnesses, Mormons and a variety of other smaller movements), and that have, within their own parameters, spawned extremist and at times dangerous religious sects.

Indeed, while writing the conclusion to this book, cultic, end-time spiritual leaders, within *Mormonism*, are being investigated and held in custody in Hawaii, for the murder of a number of individuals, including their two children.

Lori Vallow and *Chad Daybell,* believe that they have lived in previous lives and have been selected to prepare the 144,000 for the coming of Christ and that if anyone gets in the way of their mission they have the right to kill them. In fact, Lori Vallow believes that she is a "God" specially chosen to carry out this Divinely commissioned work. This is only one of the many groups within the Mormon faith who are, as it were, sects within the broader collective.

This tendency for "cults within the larger cult," can be found in the SDA faith as well, where numerous groups arise claiming that they are the ones who are being true to the teachings of Ellen G. White and the original faith. Invariably, they emphasise the extra-biblical doctrines of Mrs. White, such as what not to eat and drink, not wearing jewellery, how you should dress, entertainment and sports, etc., and more often than not separate themselves from the rest of the world in exclusive lifestyle centers or other types of closed communities.

Simply put, the fact is that nearly every denomination, by simple virtue of the fact that they teach or proclaim an interpretation of Scripture that is different in some way or other from another church, run the risk of becoming exclusive. Christianity is filled with hundreds of denominations that preach their own version of the faith—yet, they are all "Christian."

In and of itself, there is nothing wrong with believing that your understanding of scriptural truth is unique or even correct. The danger comes when a group —often on the basis of claims made by its founder or prophet—declare that THEY, above all other Christians, have received ALL the light.

What sensible believers realise is that no one group or church has ALL the truth. People from every Christian denomination, to larger or lesser degrees (God is the Judge of "degrees" and is no respector of persons) have truth, and ALL, according to their abilities and talents or unique perspective, are used by God to be a witness in this world. God's true church—His people— are to be found among all denominations.

We need to remember that Christ, in His day, often made it known that those with the strongest faith and belief were not even to be found among the chosen, Hebrew community of faith. Some of them were in fact Samaritans and Romans.

One's standing with God or the guarantee of salvation is not dependent on having all of your "theological ducks in a row"—a correct knowledge of all scriptural truth. The heart and soul of true religion is not a church denomination but a person (Jesus Christ) and a right relationship with Him. True religion, and hence salvation, is indeed a matter of the heart and soul and very personal in nature.

Beware of any entity, religious, political or otherwise, that claim they have unique status or some special corner on the market of political or religious philosophy—that their way is the only way.

Beware of any group, led by an individual or some very select or narrow, inflexible philosophy that claim that if you do not join their cause then all is lost—"join us otherwise you are doomed."

This is why, in terms of political philosophy in the

United States, it is vital to support or vote for those who are endeavouring to remain true to laws and political practices that are consistent with the Constitution and the Founder's interpretation of it.

It is for this reason that a Republican form of government, with inherent checks and balances and separation of powers—a system "of the people, by the people and for the people"—with strong accountability and equal justice, is the most sensible option.

This is also why, any religious body, that on the basis of an individual or elite group claim all truth or some sort of spiritual infallibility, automatically expose themselves as being in direct conflict to the spirit of the gospel and God's own gift of free-choice—extended to the entire human family.

And finally, this is why, in America or any other place on earth for that matter, true Christians who understand the spirit and essence of the gospel, will support and vote for institutions that extend those same types of freedoms and liberties to everyone, regardless of what they might personally choose to believe.

Exclusivity is the breeding ground for fanaticism, blind faith and self-preservation (the selfish kind).

As stated in the sub-heading of this book, *when faith without logic embraces evil without boundaries, then there is no deception, no abhorrent act or denial of reality that will not seek justification or claim absolution in the name of God and send you down the rabbit-hole to spiritual madness.*

At all costs! Avoid this dilemma!

"Well, I've had enough nonsense. I'm going home!"

SOURCES

1. *God is Going to Have to Forgive Me: Young Evangelicals Speak Out,* 1 November, 2018, *Elizabeth Dias*, New York Times
2. *Ibid*
3. *Based on data released by Pew. (https://www.adventistreview.org/u.s.-adventists-lean-more-democrat-than-republican,-survey-finds. March 3, 2016*
4. *The Great Controversy, p.423, Ellen G. White, emphasis supplied*
5. *Ellen G. White,Present Truth, August 1849, p. 21-24, emphasis supplied*
6. *Early Writings, p. 56, Ellen G. White. Quoted in, Within the Veil: Where did Christ go? by Irwin R. Gane, Ministry Magazine, emphasis supplied*
7. *From an official Seventh-day Adventist Church statement, adopted by the Council of Interchurch/Interfaith Relations of the Seventh-day Adventist Church in March 2002. Adapted and republished for the Carson bid, May 4 2015*
8. *GospelWorkers, p.391-393, Ellen G. White*
9. *Reprinted from Adventist Review, September 18 & 25, 1980 Paul A. Gordon served as undersecretary of the Ellen G. White Estate*
10. *Reprinted from Adventist Review, September 18 & 25, 1980 Paul A. Gordon served as undersecretary of the Ellen G. White Estate, emphasis supplied*
11. *Temperance, p. 255 Reprinted from Adventist Review, September18 & 25,1980 Paul A.Gordon served as undersecretary of the Ellen G. White Estate; Review and Herald, Oct.15, 1914. Reprinted from Adventist Review, September 18 & 25, 1980 Paul A. Gordon served as undersecretary of the Ellen G. White Estate*
12. *Maranatha, Ellen G. White, daily devotional compilation, p. 193, 194, emphasis supplied*
13. *Dr. Ben Carson, 12 July 2014, Avondale Memorial SDA Church, Australia. See video at: www.youtube.com/watch?v=Abdel_ luhPY. Emphasis & italics supplied*

14. *https://spectrummagazine.org/article/news/2014/10/23/im-democrat-because-my-adventist-faith*

15. *Benjamin Franklin, The Works of Benjamin Franklin, Jared Sparks, editor (Boston: Tappan, Whittemore, and Mason, 1837), Vol. V, p. 162, from "A Comparison of the Conduct of the Ancient Jews and of the Anti-Federalists in the United States of America," no date, emphasis supplied*

16. *Pastor Harold Alomia, Fatal Flirting: The Nazi State and the Seventh-day Adventist Church, Journal of Adventist Mission Studies, Vol. 6 [2010], No. 1, Art. 2, emphasis supplied*

17. *Ellen G.White, Testimonies Vol.2, p.326, 1868-1871; Counsels on Diet and Foods, page 413, paragraph 3, letter 84, 1898*

18. *In a testimony to Elders Irwin, Prescott, Waggoner, and Jones, February 21, 1899; Testimonies to the Church, Vol. 6, p. 378*

19. *Ellen G. White, Counsels on Diet and Foods, p. 70. Testimonies for the Church Vo. 3 1872-1875, emphasis supplied*

20. *Ellen White, Spirit of Prophecy Book 1, p. 78*

21. *The Great Controversy, p. 429, 430, Ellen G. White*

22. *Pastor Harold Alomia, Fatal Flirting: The Nazi State and the Seventh-day Adventist Church, Journal of Adventist Mission Studies, Vol. 6 [2010], No. 1, Art. 2, emphasis supplied*

23. *Ibid, emphasis supplied*

24. *Ibid, emphasis supplied*

25. *Ibid*

26. *Ibid*

27. *Ibid*

28. *Ibid: Religion Under National Socialism: The Case for the Seventh-day Adventist Church. Central European History 26, no. 3, Summer*

29. *Phillip Wessels to Ellen G. White, January 14, 1893*

30. *A paper presented at the Association of Seventh-day Adventist Historians meetings, April 19-22, 2007, at Oakwood College, Huntsville, Alabama by Jeff Crocombe, Senior Lecturer in Theology, Helderberg College, South Africa; du Preez and du Pre, A Century of Good Hope, 116*

31. *Ibid, p. 2*

32. *Ibid, p. 5*

33. *Ibid P. 6, as quoted by Pantalone, The Afrikaanse*

Konferensie, 307

34. *Ibid P. 6, as quoted by Pantalone, The Afrikaanse Konferensie, 309, emphasis supplied*

35. *Ellen White, Spirit of Prophecy Book 1, p. 78; Sp. Gifts. Vol. 3, p. 75 emphasis supplied*

36. *The White Elephant—In Seventh-day Adventism, Brian S. Neumann, Chapter 16, p. 688, published 2017 by Neu Creation Ministry*

37. *Uriah Smith, THE VISIONS OF MRS. E. G. WHITE, A MANIFESTATION Of SPIRITUAL GIFTS ACCORDING TO THE SCRIPTURES, p.102-105, 1868, emphasis supplied*

38. *Snook and Brinkerhoff, The Visions of E.G. White Not of God, Chapter 2, emphasis supplied*

39. *Ellen G. White, Testimonies, vol. 9, p. 210*

40. *Ellen White, Testimonies, vol. 9, p. 202*

41. *Ibid, p. 214*

42. *Ibid, p. 213*

43. *Ellen White, Manuscript 7, 1896; Selected Messages Book 2, page 343*

44. *Ellen White, Letter 36, 1912; Selected Messages, Book 2, page 344. Emphasis supplied*

45. *Ellen White, Letter 4, 1901*

46. *Ellen White, The Southern Work, p. 15*

47. *SDA General Conference President, Ted Wilson, leader of the SDA Church, in a sermon he delivered at the 2014 Annual Council on Oct 11th*

48. *The White Elephant – In Seventh-day Adventism, Brian S. Neumann, Chapter 10, published 2017 by Neu Creation Ministry*

49. *Fredericks, Richard, "A Biblical Response to Abortion" Part 1: Less Than Human?, Proclamation!, January/February, 2003, p. 10. http://www.lifeassuranceministries.org/Proclamation2003_JanFeb.pdf, emphasis supplied*

50. *Proclamation Magazine, Summer 2014, Vol. 15, Issue 2, Abortion in Adventism – Why Seventh-day Adventism Promotes Choice, Emphasis supplied*

51. *November/December 2019 issue of SDA Liberty magazine. Article by Asma T. Udin, author of the recent book, When Islam Is Not A Religion. Inside America's Fight for Religious Freedom, p. 4-7*

52. *Life and Glory, The Vital Portion of the Declaration of*

Independence, p. 383-386, July 1902 article by editor *John D. Bradley*, *The Sentinel of Christian Liberty, November/December 2019 issue of SDA Liberty magazine, p.12-15*

53. *November/December 2019 issue of SDA Liberty magazine. Article by Ed Kook: Natural Laws, The Abortion Debate Turns Legislative, p. 20-23*

54. *Ibid*

NOTE: All titles, sub-titles & sub-headings are quotes taken from Disney's Alice's Wonderland. Original version published in 1865. Authored by Chareles Lutwidge Dodgson.